A Little Boy, a Little Girl, and Their Dog Named Queenie

Harold J. McLaughlin, Ph.D.

ISBN: 979-8-88640-669-6 (sc)
ISBN: 979-8-88640-670-2 (hc)
ISBN: 979-8-88640-671-9 (e)

One Galleria Blvd., Suite 1900, Metairie, LA 70001
1-888-421-2397

CONTENTS

Introduction 1

Chapter 1   Queenie, Where Are You? 3

Chapter 2   Ilene and Jackie's Home City 6

Chapter 3   Ilene, Jackie, and Queenie's Home 10

Chapter 4   Fun and Games in the Neighborhood 25

Chapter 5   Adventures Away from Home 35

Chapter 6   Queenie Is Beginning to Act Strange 41

Chapter 7   The Secret Revealed 45

INTRODUCTION

This is a story about love and responsibility: the love of a little boy and a little girl for their dog; the dog's love for the children; the parents' love for their children and the dog; and the difficult decisions a parent must make when their children's safety is of concern. The story is also about life as it was during the early part of the last century, when bathrooms were just coming indoors and radio was a major source of entertainment.

CHAPTER 1

QUEENIE, WHERE ARE YOU?

"Queenie! Here, Queenie! Where are you, Queenie? Queenie!" cried the little boy.

"Queenie! Come here, Queenie! Where are you, girl?" called the little boy's sister.

They were searching for their dog in a field of high weeds behind their house, but she was nowhere to be found. They had been searching for her for more than a week, and they were very sad that they couldn't find her.

More than sixty years would pass before they would find out the closely guarded secret about what happened to her and why it happened.

Queenie was a three-year-old mixed breed—mostly Collie, with the rest of her lineage unknown. She was golden with splashes of white on her ears, forehead, nose, neck, and legs. She had big brown eyes and was somewhat short, and she had a very big, loving heart. She had arrived on the little boy and little girl's doorstep more than a year earlier, a stray, dirty and hungry and in need of a loving home. The little boy and girl's mother and father immediately fell in love with her. They agreed that their home would be her home too, and they named her Queenie. The name seemed to fit because once she was fed and cleaned up, she looked regal, like a queen. Queenie seemed to like her name, too, because she was quick to learn and respond to it when she was called.

Within a very short time, a bond of love developed between Queenie and the little boy and girl. Queenie was their dog, their close friend, their playmate, and their protector. Wherever they went, Queenie followed, playfully romping and jumping and barking and happily wagging her tail as they went on their way.

Jackie and Queenie

The little boy and little girl could not stray too far from their house because Ilene was only eight, and Jackie was only five. They had a very close brother-sister relationship and loved each other very much. When they played away from home, Ilene watched over her small brother just as a mother would, making sure he did not get into any situations where he could get hurt.

Jackie and Ilene

CHAPTER 2

ILENE AND JACKIE'S HOME CITY

I lene and Jackie lived in a small city named Dearborn in the state of Michigan. Dearborn is in southeastern Michigan and is one of the several cities that adjoin Detroit. Detroit is often called the Automobile Capital of the World because it is here where many of the world's automobiles are built. Dearborn was made very famous by one of its early residents, Henry Ford, who built his huge automobile factory there and named it the Rouge Plant.

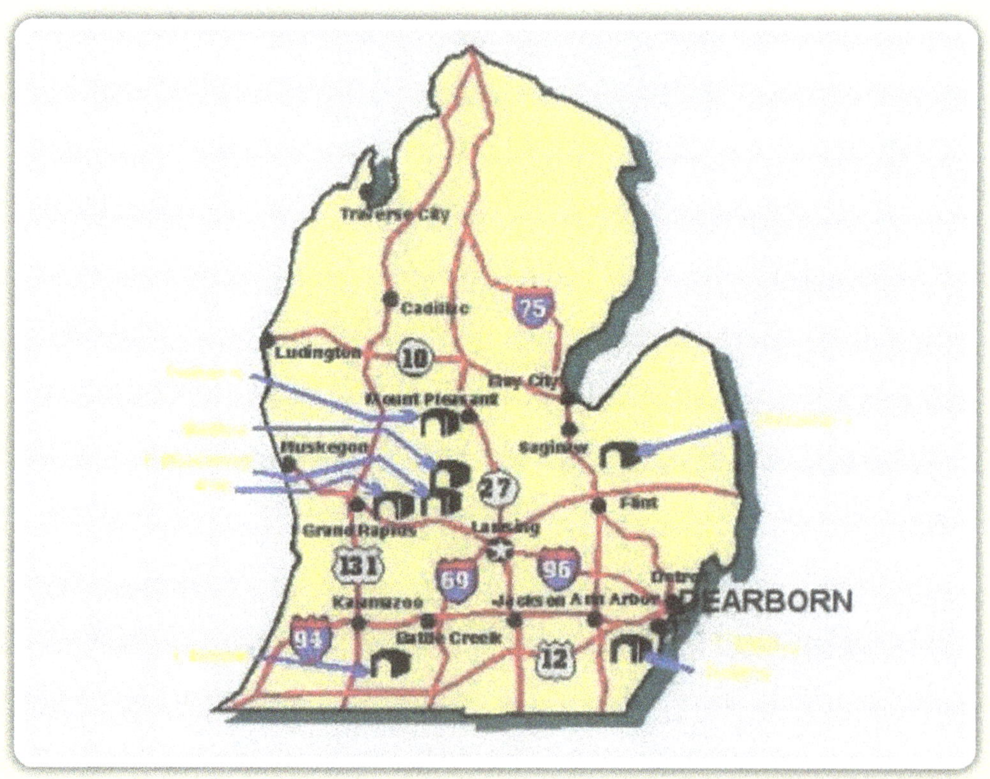

Map of the lower peninsula of Michigan, noting the location of Dearborn

Dearborn was just starting to grow from a farming community to a city in 1938, when Ilene and Jackie were growing up. Many new homes and apartments were being built for the families who moved into this growing city. Many of the fathers, and some mothers, worked in Ford's huge automobile factory. But even with the construction, there were still a lot of vacant fields with thick brush, high grass, weeds, picker bushes, and marshes behind Ilene and Jackie's house, where they would play games, many of which they made up themselves, and Queenie would roam, explore, and hide.

Many freight trains ran through Dearborn's neighborhoods, and their tracks crossed one of the city's main streets, Schaffer Road, near Ilene and Jackie's house, and stretched for miles in the field behind it. Several times each day, a steam-powered locomotive giving off billowing clouds of white and gray smoke pulled its cars filled with freight of all kinds far into the field behind their house and to cities beyond. The train tracks, the train's engine, and the freight cars made it a very dangerous place for small children, especially if they were wandering around the train tracks by themselves, without adults watching them. But Jackie and Ilene did wander near the train tracks without their mother or father knowing, and they called out for their lost friend, "Here, Queenie! Come home, Queenie!" Fortunately, Ilene and Jackie were not harmed, but no, Queenie did not answer their call.

A steam locomotive billowing steam clouds

The field behind Jackie and Ilene's house was also home to small creeks and deep holes in the ground that filled with muddy water when it rained. It was also home to large field rats that were a danger to children and adults alike. But little Ilene and Jackie, both wearing bib overalls, were not concerned about or even aware of these dangers as they wandered through the field covered with high weeds and picker bushes that scratched at their pant legs. They continued calling out, "Here, Queenie! Come home, Queenie!"

Queenie was not there or anywhere near, but Ilene and Jackie did not know that and wouldn't know it for more than sixty years. Every day for two weeks, with tears in their eyes and with heavy hearts, they continued to look and call out, "Here, Queenie! Come home, Queenie!"

Ilene and Jackie walking in high weeds

CHAPTER 3

ILENE, JACKIE, AND QUEENIE'S HOME

Ilene and Jackie lived in a small house on Schaffer Road with their younger brother, Carl, who was only three years old, and their mother and father, Josephine and Buster. Josie (as she liked to be called) and Buster were young themselves, but they were good parents who were filled with much love and concern for their three small children and for Queenie. They felt lucky that Queenie had joined their family and was so attached to their children. They knew the children were safe when Queenie was with them.

In 1938, the United States was still in what was called the Great Depression. Millions of people throughout the country were out of work, and many of those people—mothers, fathers, and their children—did not have food to eat or homes to live in. Government officials throughout the country, including the president, state governors, mayors, and city council members from cities across the country, did what they could to help people find work, places to live, and food to eat. Dearborn's mayor and city council helped by allowing small garage homes to be built because most people didn't have money to build bigger homes, and the people needed places to live where jobs were available. Garage homes were just that; they were a little larger than one of today's two-car garages. The Ford Motor Company had factory jobs for some people, and many of those people lived in these small, affordable homes. Ilene and Jackie's family home was one of these small garage homes.

Ilene and Jackie's garage home

Ilene and Jackie's family was luckier than most because their father had a steady job as a laborer with the city of Dearborn. It didn't pay much, eighty-five cents an hour, or thirty-eight dollars per week for a forty-hour week, but it was steady work, and that was more than most people earned during the Great Depression. Automobile factory workers earned a little more than that, but their jobs were often eliminated when automobile sales were weak. Ilene and Jackie's father considered his family to be very lucky to have what they had.

The rooms in Ilene and Jackie's house were very small: a kitchen, a living room, two bedrooms on the first floor, and an unfinished attic that served as a bedroom for Jackie and Carlie. Josie and Buster nicknamed Jack and Carl Jackie and Carlie because they felt those names fit the children better.

When their house was first built, it did not have indoor running water, flush toilets, or even a bathtub, but that was not unusual for that period in Dearborn's history. Water had to be hand pumped from a well in the ground and put into pails, then carried into the house for drinking, cooking, and washing.

Hand water pump

A very small house called an outhouse was where the family toilet was. It was usually located outside and far away from the main house and was positioned over a deep hole in the ground. Inside, there was a seat with a hole cut into it to sit on. Going to the toilet was a great inconvenience, especially during the winter months when it was cold and there was deep snow on the ground. People had to first dress for the cold outdoors with heavy coats, hats, leggings, and boots, then trudge through the deep snow and ice to the outhouse. Once there, they had to partially undress to sit on a very cold wooden seat to complete their business. It was a very uncomfortable experience they repeated several times each day.

Toilet paper was a luxury, and many people couldn't afford to buy it, so a substitute was used. Often the substitute was a page from a *Sears and Roebuck* catalog, a magazine, a newspaper, or another similar material.

Grandma Martha at the outhouse

Taking a bath without running water was not easy. Because of its difficulty, it was usually done only once a week, and quite often, more than one person would share the same bathwater. A big silver-colored metal tub was used as a bathtub. Water was heated, usually on the kitchen stove, then poured into the tub. When the first person completed his or her bath, the next person would take theirs. When the bath was over, the tub was taken outside, and the water was dumped on the ground. The bathers typically changed their underwear after their once-a-week bath.

Metal tub—type used for bathing

Buster's mother and father, Martha and Dale, and their four sons and two daughters lived in Buster and Josie's garage house before them. When Dale, Martha, and their family lived in this house, there was no indoor running water or flush toilets or bathtubs, but they were eventually added before they moved out. The very small bathroom, just off the kitchen, was only big enough to hold a bathtub, a toilet, and a sink. When today's standards are considered, it was amazing that eight people could live in that small house without running water or an indoor bathroom, but they managed.

Entry into the house was several steps up to a small porch that led to the back door.

Josie with Ilene, Jackie, and Carlie at the back porch

During the spring, summer, and fall months, Queenie was often found sleeping on this porch because she was an outside dog and was allowed inside only during the daytime. During the winter months, Queenie usually slept in her doghouse in the backyard. It was lined with rugs and blankets to help keep her warm. Queenie spent most of her time outdoors because Josie did not like to clean the hair that Queenie always left behind on the furniture and floors. Even so, Queenie did spend some time in the house, playing with the three children, but under Josie's watchful eye.

The small garage home was heated by a coal-fired stove that sat on a silver-colored metal tray on the floor, positioned to one side of the small living room. It looked like a Ben Franklin stove but without a big potbelly. It had smoother lines than a Franklin stove and was dark maroon. A metal pail with an oval carrying handle, silver in color, was used to haul and store the coal that fueled the stove's fire. It handily sat next to the stove. During the winter months, when Queenie was allowed inside the house, her favorite place to lie was in front of this stove. Ilene, Jackie, and Carlie were often found lying with their heads on Queenie's belly, in front of the stove. They loved to do that, to be close to their friend and protector. Queenie liked it too!

Ben Franklin–type stove

Queenie lying by the Ben Franklin stove

A large Philco radio sat on the floor on the left side of the living room, just inside the doorway leading to the kitchen. Television, Game Boys, CDs and CD players, MP3 players, computers, computer games, cell phones, and other electronic marvels had not yet been invented, and radio was the main source of entertainment for adults and children. Jackie would often lie on the floor in front of the Philco radio and listen to stories about his heroes, the Lone Ranger and Jack Armstrong, the all-American boy, win their battles over the forces of evil. He often imagined himself as the Lone Ranger or Jack

Armstrong doing battle with these evil forces himself while lying there on the floor with his arm around his best friend, Queenie, who lay there beside him. If Jackie needed help conquering these evil forces, Queenie would be there to help him. Jackie would say to Queenie, "We can do it, can't we, girl? We can beat the bad guys—you and me together." Queenie would respond with a big "Woof! Woof!" That was good enough for Jackie!

Philco floor model radio

Mounted on top of the doorway between the kitchen and living room was a baby swing, the kind that had elastic bands that allowed Carlie to jump up and down in the swing, which helped him to learn to stand by himself. A daybed was located on one wall of the living room, near a window, and Jackie would take his afternoon nap there, with his friend and protector, Queenie, lying by his side. Jackie was able to drift off to sleep better with Queenie by his side. She didn't seem to mind because she liked to nap too, beside her friend.

Every Sunday at five o'clock, Buster would turn on the Philco radio to listen to his favorite program, *The Shadow.* It was a mystery program, and the hero who fought evildoers was the Shadow. He had control over men's minds so that they could not see him. He used that gift to solve crimes and bring the evildoers to justice. The whole family would listen to the program, and when the evildoer was brought to justice, Queenie would bark her "Woof! Woof!" of approval as though she knew what was going on. Following this program, Josie would serve rice pudding or white cake with milk as everyone's Sunday treat. Queenie was left out of this treat because sweets make dogs sick.

Even though the kitchen was small and decorated with few pieces of furniture, it was a friendly place where everyone seemed to gather. It had a small gas stove with four match-lighted burners that were turned on and off with white, porcelain, round handles. In the kitchen's center was a small wooden table with four worn, matching chairs and an infant's high chair, providing places for Buster, Josie, Ilene, Jackie, and Carlie to sit. On the walls were several small cupboards used to store dishes, pots, pans, and cooking spices.

Josie was especially proud of her kitchen because she had a new, modern refrigerator that replaced her icebox. The icebox was just that, an insulated box that held a fifty-pound block of ice with room for perishable food storage. Ice was delivered by the ice man every few days and was used use to keep the food in the box cool to prevent it from spoiling. Ilene, Jackie, and Queenie had looked forward to the ice man coming because he gave them ice chips to suck on.

There was not much room for anything else in the kitchen, except for a lot of love given by Josie and Buster to each other and to their children and by Queenie to all of them.

Josie's small kitchen with a stove and table and chairs

Josie and Buster's bedroom had a double bed and a dresser with a matching chest of drawers, overlaid with veneer, light brown in color, and with even a lighter color running through it. They treasured this set and kept it throughout their many years of marriage. Queenie was not allowed in this room. She knew it and never tried to enter. Josie had to tell Queenie only once, "Queenie, don't ever go in here, or you'll not come into this house again, even on cold winter days." Queenie was smart in ways such as that, and she didn't want to abuse her indoor privileges.

Josie and Buster's small bedroom

Ilene's bedroom was sparsely furnished with an old twin bed, which had a badly scratched oak headboard, and an unmatched and marred dresser with six drawers to hold her clothes. It wasn't much, but she was glad to have it, and it was her own space in her small house. Ilene did share it once in a while with Queenie but only when her mother and father were not around or not looking, because she didn't belong there either. Ilene would say to Queenie, "Come on in, Queenie. It's OK. Mom and Dad are not around. I'll let you in my room, but you have to be quiet and not bark." Queenie would then quietly slip into Ilene's room without so much as a quiet "Woof. Woof." She knew better.

A poorly lit, second-story, unfinished attic with one small bed was the bedroom for Jackie and Carlie. It was a very spooky place, but their mother and father had no other place to put them. Each night, as the two small boys lay in bed in their darkened room, two pairs of soft, dark, watchful eyes that missed nothing peeked from beneath their blankets. They often thought they saw and heard a bogeymen and other frightening hobgoblins hiding behind the roof support timbers and behind the redbrick chimney of their attic bedroom. Jackie and Carlie thought these creatures were out to scare them and do terrible things to them. Many dark nights, they wished their best friend, Queenie, could be with them so they could curl up in her protective coat of brown fur, but Queenie had to sleep outdoors. They believed that Queenie could easily fight off any of those frightening hobgoblins all by herself because no bogeyman could scare her. However, their mother and father did not allow Queenie to be with them at night, so they had to be brave and join together to fight them all by themselves. Since these bogeymen and hobgoblins were only in their imaginations, these imaginary creatures never moved from behind their roof supports or chimney hiding places, so the boys were safe. Since the hobgoblins didn't move, and terrible things did not happen to them, their covers would be lowered, and then the two pairs of soft, dark, watchful eyes would close, and they would drift off to a peaceful sleep. Each night for many years, this search for imaginary bogeymen and hobgoblins was repeated.

Jackie and Carlie in bed, peeking out and looking at specters

From the back porch steps, a path led to a small coal shed perhaps forty yards away. To keep the house heated in the winter, Jackie's father took the coal bucket from its resting place in the living room and walked to the coal shed in the backyard, filled it to the brim, and returned it to the house. This was a daily ritual during the cold fall and winter months because, to keep the house warm, the stove had to be fed its ration of coal from the storage bucket every few hours. A filled pail of coal was needed each day to do this. When Jackie was about five years old, he was allowed to carry the bucket to the shed all by himself, fill it half-full, then drag it back to the house. He felt proud and very grown-up doing this necessary choir for the rest of the family. Since the bucket was almost as big as he was, he couldn't lift it when it was only half-full, so dragging it was the only way he could get it back to the house. When he got it to the house, Buster or Josie would help him lift the half-filled bucket up the back steps. They expressed much joy over Jackie's contribution because it showed he was growing up and becoming a responsible member of the family.

Jackie was not alone on his daily treks to the coal shed because his best friend, Queenie, was with him, at his heels, jumping with the same joy that he himself felt in his accomplishment. She would also grab the bucket edge with her teeth to help Jackie drag it back to the house. As she followed him back to the house, her tail was always wagging, showing her approval. Since Queenie was always at his heels during his walk to and from the coal shed, and since the shed was always closed, this was not a place where she could hide.

Jackie carrying a large pail of coal with Queenie by his side

CHAPTER 4

FUN AND GAMES IN THE NEIGHBORHOOD

On one side of Jackie and Ilene's little garage house was a vacant lot, and next to it was a large, two-story house that was painted white. A wide gravel driveway and a small field of high weeds separated the two houses. Ilene and Jackie's Uncle Clyde, Aunt Evelyn, and their four children, Glen, Donnie, Truman, and their sister "Sisy," lived there. Clyde was Buster's brother. The three boys and girl often played with Ilene, Jackie, Carlie, and of course Queenie, who liked them as friends too. Because of her loving and gentle ways, Queenie was liked by almost everyone. Queenie, in return, liked almost everyone too.

Next to the big white house were many vacant lots filled with high weeds and one big and very old apple tree that stood by itself, alone in a sea of weeds. Its branches were scraggly and knurled because they had never been pruned. Apple trees need to be pruned each year if they are expected to grow big, healthy, juicy apples. Instead, it produced small apples, red and white in color, always full of worms, and usually not fit to eat. During the late summer when the apples were ripe, Jackie would often climb this scraggly old apple tree in search of good, healthy red apples without worms to take home for the family to eat. Queenie was always there, waiting beneath the tree, standing guard in case Jackie fell. If he did, she could run for help if he was hurt. At times, his search was successful, and he was able to take home a basket of apples. This made his mother very happy because, with them, she could make her family an apple pie or some other delicious dessert. This of course made Jackie very proud because now he felt like he was helping the rest of the family.

Two-story, white, wooden house with an apple tree beside it

One of Jackie's prized possessions was his black metal car, whose front end looked very much like a very small 1920s-model truck. It was made to fit a small boy such as Jackie and was equipped with large, rubber-covered wheels, pedals to make it go, and a steering wheel to give it direction. Jackie enjoyed driving it around his backyard, on the driveway beside his house, and on the sidewalk in front of his house. The sidewalk led to a gas station about ten city lots from the big, white-painted house next door. He often pedaled his car to the gas station, where he pretended to fill it with gasoline, just like his father did with his car. Queenie of course would follow alongside Jackie's car, jumping and barking with excitement, her tail in a constant wag to show her happiness and that she was glad to be with him.

The gas pumps had big, clear, glass bowls on top of them, with lines circling the bowl and a number next to each line indicating the number of gallons measured at that point. An electric pump filled the bowl with the number of gallons of gasoline a customer wanted to buy. When the bowl was filled to its proper level, the gasoline would flow from the bowl to the pump's hose into the car's gasoline tank. Jackie would pull his car next to one of the gas pumps, and he and Queenie would stare up at the bowl, imagining it filling with gasoline. Then he would take the pump handle with both hands and pretend it was filling his little, black, metal car with gasoline. The gas station attendant was always nearby and watched Jackie and Queenie to make sure no harm came to them. He enjoyed watching them each time they paid his station a visit.

Jackie and his car at the gas station

Next door to Jackie and Ilene's house, on its other side, was a two-story house with brown asphalt siding. A family named Jamison lived in it, and they had a young girl named Irene and a small boy Donnie. Irene was the same age as Ilene, and Donnie was the same age as Jackie. They, too, became fast friends with Queenie. Their backyard had no grass or flowers and adjoined Queenie's yard, which did have some grass and a few flowers. An old outhouse sat in the backyard of this two-story house, but it had not been used for several years because this family had indoor running water and a toilet installed, but it had no bathtub. This family took their weekly baths in an old, big, dented, silver-colored tub they filled with hot water they heated on their kitchen stove. The tub was placed on the kitchen floor near the back door, close to their back porch. When the tub was filled with hot water, they got as much of their body in as would fit without spilling the water on the floor, then soaked and washed until they were clean. When they were through, they dragged the tub a few feet through the kitchen door, to the edge of the back porch, and tipped up one end until the water flowed out the bottom onto their grassless backyard. When it was Donnie's turn for his bath, he would holler and cry loudly so all the neighbors could hear, because he didn't like to take baths. He thought his hollering and crying would make his tormentors quit, but it never did. He got his bath and a change of clean underwear every week. Queenie stayed away from these people on their bath day, especially around the porch when the tub was emptied, because she didn't want a bath either.

Heating bathwater on the kitchen stove

Ilene, Jackie, Carlie, and their cousins, Glen, Donnie, Truman, and Sisy, and neighbors Irene and Donnie all became very good friends and played together constantly. Queenie, of course, was always included in their games. Since television had not yet been invented, the children had to invent their own games. They also played some games their parents had played many years before. One of them was called enie-iny-over—the ball is coming over. In this game, half the children would stand in the front of Jackie and Ilene's small house, and the other half would stand in back of the house. One of the children on one side of the house would shout, "Enie-iny-over! The ball is coming over!" Then they would throw the ball over the house to the other side. A player on the other side of the house would try to guess where it was coming from and attempt to catch it before it hit the ground. Queenie, of course, was a part of the game and would try to catch it before any of the children could. Queenie often won, but the children didn't seem to mind at all because she was fun to play with. They enjoyed watching her bark and jump with joy when the ball came over to their side. When the ball was thrown to the other side, Queenie would race there, too, often getting there before the ball did. The children would holler and scream with glee at Queenie's antics.

The other game they often played was the old standby, hide-and-seek, played by many people over many generations. In this game, one child was *it* and blindfolded his or her eyes while the other children hid. After a short while, the it person had to find the other players in their hiding spot. This game didn't work well with Queenie present because she would always give Ilene, Jackie, and Carlie's hiding place away by running to it and barking loudly so the it player would easily find them. The children didn't seem to mind this because they all enjoyed Queenie's part in the game.

Ilene, Jackie, Carlie, and Queenie playing hide-and-seek

Next to the Jamisons' house was another just like it, occupied by Ilene, Jackie, and Carlie's grandparents, Grandpa Dale and Grandma Martha. A very wide gravel driveway separated the two homes. This driveway also curved around in back of the children's grandparents' house, past an empty lot, and connected to Haggerty Road. Ruts in this gravel driveway, made by cars between the house and Haggerty Road, always filled with water after a rain. These muddy puddles provided many hours of fun for Ilene, Jackie, Carlie, and many of the other four grandchildren, as well as Irene and Donnie, who ran through them, getting their shoes and feet wet and muddy. Queenie, of course, enjoyed this game, too, and was right behind the children, barking, jumping, and wagging her tail as she got her paws and legs wet. The splashing water turned her light brown coat a dirty brown. Both she and the children enjoyed the game, but the children's mothers and grandmother were left cleaning up the mess. They didn't mind though because they enjoyed watching the children and Queenie having a good time.

Ilene, Jackie, and friends running through a muddy rut in the driveway

Behind this house was an old apple tree that also had very twisted, scraggly, and knurled branches, and each year the tree grew small, odd-shaped red apples that were full of worms. None of them could be eaten. This tree, however, did give the children something to climb, with great joy … when their mothers and grandmother were not watching. Sometimes Grandpa Dale would fashion a swing by tying one end of a rope to an old car tire and the other rope end to a big branch on the tree. The children would put their legs through the tire and then sit on it. Then Grandpa would push them until their toes reached the sky. "Yeah!" they would cry. "This is great fun." Queenie, too, would get her turn, sometimes by lying on the tire and being pushed by one of the children or by being held by one of the children as they were being pushed high into the sky. Queenie and the children loved feeling the wind on their faces as the tire swing took them back and forth, from the ground to the sky and back again. "What fun!" squealed the children, heard above Queenie barking her approval. Mother and grandmother would hold their breath and close their eyes as the children did this, fearing that harm would come to the children, but it never did.

Jackie on the tire swing

Also behind this house and across the gravel driveway was a rickety, old, wooden garage that resembled a barn more than a garage. In fact, it probably was a horse barn when the property was a farm. Jackie and Ilene's grandfather Dale had an old Ford Model T type of touring car permanently parked in this garage. The car had no roof, and its engine was started (when it was capable of running) by turning a crank mounted on the car's front, underneath its radiator. The car only occasionally ran, and when it did, Grandpa Dale would park it in the driveway so Jackie and Ilene and their cousins could play in it.

It provided them with many hours of fun as they pretended to drive it. They would sit on the car's old, leather, front bench seat, with one of them behind the old, wooden steering wheel, pretending to drive. Queenie, of course, was sitting there, too, beside them, looking very pleased, with her head held high, as though she was really driving down the street with the wind in her face.

Ilene, Jackie, Queenie, and friend in Grandpa Dale's old touring car

CHAPTER 5

ADVENTURES AWAY FROM HOME

The sidewalk in front of Ilene's house along Schaffer Road also led past the Jamisons' house, their grandparents' house, and an empty lot, then to Haggerty Road. Across Haggerty Road and past several empty lots and a few buildings was another big building that was a restaurant and bar. Ilene and Jackie's other grandfather, Joe, owned it. Joe was Josie's father. He was also a big, happy, gentle man who loved children, especially his grandchildren. Joe had immigrated to the United States from Germany thrity-five years earlier in search of a better life for the family he would have later in life. When he was growing up in Germany, Joe was able to attend only grammar school, but that didn't stop his success. He was a resourceful and talented man. He worked very hard to learn many trades. He was a barber, a cook, a butcher, and a very good businessman.

Joe owned a restaurant with a bar, and he named it the Alps Café, because he wanted something to remind him of the Alpine mountain range in Germany he so loved. He had a big painting of the Alpine mountains hanging on one wall of his café. He decorated his café just like those in Germany. A large dance floor was surrounded by many small, round tables with wicker-back chairs. A bandstand was at one end of the dance floor, and when the band was playing, it played German polka music that sounded like "Oompah, oompah!" One of the band members played an accordion that made the polka music sound just right.

Alps Café dance floor and accordion player

Grandpa Joe's café also had dinner tables and chairs for people who wanted to have a meal of homemade old-fashioned German food. Homemade German sausage was one of the favorite dishes he served. Joe made the sausage himself and would drape the long strands of sausage links across and around the kitchen ceiling to cure. They gave off a wonderful bouquet of spice odors that made you hungry just walking by the kitchen.

A long bar to the left of the entry door was where beer and other drinks were served. On the left side of the bar were several big, glass-enclosed boxes. One held potato chips, another held popcorn, and yet another held pretzels.

When the weather was sunny, Ilene and Jackie's mother let them walk down the sidewalk, across Haggerty Road, to her father's restaurant. Queenie, of course, went along, too, walking beside them as their friend and protector.

Her tail wagged back and forth to show she was happy because she was with them and needed. The three of them made a pretty picture as they walked down the sidewalk, the two holding hands, with Queenie walking beside them. The children looked like cute ragamuffins, she in her plain, faded blue-gray, sleeveless, and wrinkled dress and him in a short-sleeve shirt and short, blue, wrinkled pants held up with suspenders. Both wore sandals on their feet. When Ilene and Jackie went into the restaurant, Queenie happily stayed outside, lying on the sidewalk and guarding the entrance until they came out.

Jackie, Ilene, and Queenie in front of the Alps Café

Grandfather Joe was always very pleased to see Ilene and Jackie when they went into his restaurant. He always lifted them onto the high barstools and proudly introduced them to his customers. He let them have as much popcorn, potato chips, and pretzels as they could eat. He also gave them a cold soft drink called Rock & Rye to help wash down the popcorn, potato chips, and pretzels, as much as they wanted. He was a good grandfather, and they loved him very much.

Haggerty Street crossed Schaffer Road, and three blocks away was Lowery School, where Ilene was in the third grade and Jackie was in kindergarten. Jackie didn't like to go to school, and every morning when it was time to go, he would run outside and hide, sometimes behind the coal shed, other times around his grandparents' or the Jamisons' house or even his aunt and uncle's house. Josie would run outside after him to make him go to school, but she was not always able to catch him. She would call for Queenie to help. "Queenie, Queenie!" she would call. "Find Jackie. He must go to school." Queenie would call out in her friendly "Woof! Woof!" and bound off, sniffing the air to find him. With Queenie on his trail, he had no place to hide, as she would find him. Josie would go to his hiding place and grab him by his ear. Then she and Queenie would walk him to Schaffer Road, cross it with him, and send him on his way to school, with Queenie by his side to make sure he got there. Somehow Queenie always knew when school was out because she was always there to greet Ilene and Jackie and walk them safely home. Perhaps she heard the school bell ring and knew that was when school was over and they would be coming home.

Jackie and Queenie running home when school was out

Queenie also saved Jackie's life. One summer day, Jackie went into the field behind his house, where some older boys had built a large fire out of scrap wood and paper. Jackie was not supposed to play with fire. He would learn that lesson the hard way. That day, he was wearing long pants, and he got too close to the flame, and it caught his left pants leg on fire. Queenie saw what was happening, and she gripped his right pant leg in her powerful teeth and pulled Jackie to safety. She released him and barked to get the attention of the older boys, who ran over and put out the fire on Jackie's pants. Queenie then ran to Jackie's house and continued barking until Josie came out to see what was going on. Queenie ran back and forth, trying to get Josie to follow him. She finally understood and followed Queenie to Jackie and his smoldering pants leg. Josie ripped his pants leg open to reveal a very serious burn. Josie carried Jackie home, and Queenie followed.

At home, Josie called Buster at work, and he came home to take her and Jackie to a local doctor. After the doctor examined Jackie and cleaned and bandaged his burns, he said Jackie's leg burn was very serious. It would take several weeks or even months to heal, but he was lucky to have had Queenie there to save him. Queenie was declared a hero for her quick action. Buster felt Queenie deserved something special for her bravery and quick action, so he rewarded her with a big hug and a juicy steak. "Thank you, Queenie, for saving Jackie," said Buster as Queenie munched on her steak.

The doctor was right. It did take several weeks for Jackie's burn to heal. He spent those weeks in Ilene's bed in the downstairs bedroom. Ilene had to sleep with Carlie in the attic bedroom. Fortunately, Jackie was not alone, as Josie allowed Queenie to lie on the floor beside his bed to keep him company and watch over him. Jackie learned one important lesson from that experience: don't play with fire! Fire is dangerous, and Queenie or someone else might not be around to save him if he played with it and caught on fire again.

Jackie on fire and Queenie the heroine

CHAPTER 6

QUEENIE IS BEGINNING TO ACT STRANGE

One day, Ilene and Jackie noticed Queenie was getting a lot of attention from other dogs and was not paying attention to them. In fact, Queenie preferred the other dogs' company and would not come when called. Queenie was getting many new friends, other dogs, four or five at a time and all boy dogs. Ilene and Jackie wondered what was happening because Queenie wanted to be with these other dogs rather than with them. She didn't want to follow them around as much as she used to. Ilene and Jackie wondered what they had done to make Queenie not like them as she had before.

Jackie and Queenie with three other dogs

They first asked each other, and then Ilene asked their mother and father, "What have we done to Queenie to make her mad at us? She won't come when we call her. She wants to be with the other dogs and not with us. What can we do to make her like us again so we can be friends again?"

Their father said, "Queenie is now a grown-up dog. She is three years old, and in terms of people years, that is twenty-one, and she is ready to have a family of her own. When girl dogs reach this age or even two years old, they want to have puppies, and they search out the best boy dog to be the father of their puppies. Just like people, dogs want to have the very best mates for their children. Boy dogs will seek out girl dogs who are ready to have puppies. When girl dogs are ready to have puppies, they give out a scent that boy dogs can smell. This scent attracts the boy dogs to the girl dogs so they can choose who they want as the father of their puppies.

This scent period is called *heat*, and it can last for up to three weeks, during which time the girl dogs will select their mate. After they mate, it will take about eight weeks for the girl dog to have her puppies. Girl dogs can do this as often as twice per year. So you see, Ilene and Jackie, Queenie ignoring you in favor of other dogs has nothing to do with you at all. It is natural for her to do this. In three weeks, if she isn't going to have puppies, she will be back to normal and will be loving and playing with you just like before. If she is going to have puppies, she may continue to act strange until after she has them, and then she will want you two to help care for them."

Ilene and Jackie felt much better after their father explained that to them. "See, Jackie," said Ilene. "She will love us and play with us again soon, so we'll just have to be patient."

Josie and Buster had also noticed Queenie's strange behavior and were concerned that the male dogs in her company could be a danger to their children, and Queenie might not be able to defend them if one or more of the dogs attacked the children.

A few days after these concerns were noticed and discussed by Ilene and Jackie's father and mother, Queenie disappeared. She just didn't come home for dinner one night. Jackie's and Ilene's hearts were broken. They wondered what they had done to make Queenie mad at them and not love them to the point she would not come home. They thought that Queenie might be somewhere in the neighborhood, making a home for her and her new puppies that she might have in eight weeks.

For more than two weeks after Queenie disappeared, Ilene and Jackie looked and called for Queenie all over their neighborhood. "Here, Queenie! Come here, Queenie!" called Jackie.

"Come home, Queenie!" cried Ilene.

They searched and called for Queenie in and around the coal shed in their backyard; the field in back of their house; the white, two-story house where their aunt and uncle with their four children lived; around the base of the big apple tree next to their aunt and uncle's house; the gas station where the little boy imagined he filled his black, metal, miniature automobile with gasoline; the abandoned outhouse behind the house next door; the garage at their grandparents' house; and the sidewalk leading to their other grandfather's restaurant. Finally, they stopped looking and calling for her. Their hearts were broken because they believed their friend, companion, playmate, and protector no longer loved them since she did not come home.

Ilene and Jackie searching for Queenie in the field near the train tracks

No longer did Jackie call out, "Here, Queenie! Come here, Queenie."
No longer did Ilene call out, "Come home, Queenie."
Their voices were now silent for Queenie.

CHAPTER 7

THE SECRET REVEALED

Many years passed, and Jackie and Ilene grew up to be adults. They married and had children, and their children had children, and their children had dogs of their own. However, in all the years that passed, Ilene and Jackie never stopped thinking about their Queenie and why she had not come home.

It was during these later years that Jackie and Ilene discovered what really happened to their beloved Queenie. An older aunt, their mother's sister, Helen, had known the truth all these years and assumed Ilene and Jackie had also known it, but they had not. Aunt Helen told them that when Queenie had all of the male dogs following her around, their mother and father grew very concerned for their safety. They were afraid Queenie could not protect them if they were attacked by one of the other dogs. This greatly distressed their parents, to the point that they decided it was best to call the dog pound and have the dog catcher take Queenie away, which is what they did. They reasoned it was far better to break Jackie's and Ilene's hearts, knowing that they would be broken for only a short time, than to have them physically hurt by angry dogs. It was a very difficult decision for them to make, because they did not want to hurt their children in any way or to hurt Queenie, but they did what they had to do. After all, that is what parents are for, to make difficult choices and difficult decisions for those who are too young to do it for themselves.

Jackie and Ilene thanked their aunt Helen for giving them this information. Now they knew it was not because Queenie did not love them that she did not come home; it was because of their parents' love for them.

This former little boy and former little girl hope there is a heaven for dogs because when it is their turn to leave this earth and they too go to heaven, they want to once again see their beloved Queenie to thank her for all the love, friendship, and protection she gave them when they were growing up. When they also see their parents in heaven, Jackie and Ilene want to thank them for their concern for their safety when they were little and the difficult decision they had to make in having Queenie taken away.

There will be even more happiness in heaven when this is done!

Buster, Josie, Ilene, Jackie, Carlie,
and Queenie at the pearly gates of heaven